IMAGES of America
SOUTH AND EAST CHELMSFORD

This card, postmarked August 4, 1943, shows the archaic spelling of Heart Pond perpetuated on official maps and postcards until around 1950. Officially, the pond is named for its shape and not for Hart families in Chelmsford and Carlisle or the five-year-old male red deer called a hart. On the other hand, if one were a Chelmsford "townie," they only knew it as Baptist Pond. (Donald MacGillivray.)

ON THE COVER: For a short time after 1937, Charles Simpson Jr. owned all three stores in South Chelmsford village: 1 Common Street, shown here; 320 Acton Road, two doors down; and 321 Acton Road, across the street. Charles Jr. demolished this store, built in 1909 for Lyman Byam, and erected a house on the site around 1940. Soon afterward, he converted the store at 320 Acton Road into a house. (Kathleen Connors.)

IMAGES of America
SOUTH AND EAST CHELMSFORD

Fred Merriam
Foreword by Pamela Byam Rivard

ARCADIA
PUBLISHING

Copyright © 2020 by Fred Merriam
ISBN 978-1-4671-0472-2

Published by Arcadia Publishing
Charleston, South Carolina

Library of Congress Control Number: 2019949048

For all general information, please contact Arcadia Publishing:
Telephone 843-853-2070
Fax 843-853-0044
E-mail sales@arcadiapublishing.com
For customer service and orders:
Toll-Free 1-888-313-2665

Visit us on the Internet at www.arcadiapublishing.com

This book is dedicated to the residents of South and East Chelmsford who have pride in their community and curiosity about its past.

Contents

Foreword 6

Acknowledgments 7

Introduction 8

1. Kate's Corner 9
2. Heart Pond 19
3. Farming Life 41
4. Nature's Fury 81
5. Gone Forever 89
6. East Chelmsford 107

Foreword

In May 2018, I attended the Chelmsford Historical Society annual dinner meeting, where the Guardian Award was presented to Fred Merriam for his outstanding contribution to the preservation of our town's history. He gave a brief talk about the work he did for the town that earned him the prestigious award. As a member of the society's board of directors, he wasn't eligible for the award, but the board secretly voted to make an exception in this case. In the talk, he declared that four books in his all-consuming second career as an author was quite enough (three books on Chelmsford and one on York Beach, Maine). He wanted to spend more time with his wife, Carol, and at their condominium in York Beach. I was happy for Fred and approached him with the intention of congratulating and expressing my gratitude for all he did for our town. Instead, I found myself saying, "Fred, you can't retire. You wrote books on Chelmsford, North Chelmsford, and West Chelmsford, but you haven't written one about South Chelmsford." I live in South Chelmsford, where my Byam ancestors settled in the mid-1600s and felt that our stories needed telling. He laughed in a way that made me believe my not-too-subtle suggestion was going nowhere, but the following night he called me: "Here's the deal. I'll write a book on South Chelmsford and East Chelmsford, too, if you help me." He was hooked, and so was I. Two weeks later, we began.

—Pamela Byam Rivard

ACKNOWLEDGMENTS

Starting a project like this without knowing if there are enough high-quality photographs out there to do it justice takes a leap of faith. Fortunately, one contact led to another and another, and it all worked out. Present generations of the Byam, Lewis, Parlee, Sousa, and Waite families shared their history and photographs and reviewed content for accuracy. A collection of South Chelmsford photographs and postcards was unexpectedly discovered on an unrelated visit with Donald MacGillivray. Henry Parlee had an old trunk in the attic that had several envelopes of Dutton, McHugh, and Parlee family negatives that had never been developed or seen.

Photographs are credited to Kevin Cantrell, Kathleen Connors, Joan Crandall, Christopher Ferreira, Gary Frascarelli, Deborah Jones, Monica Kent, Don MacGillivray, Isabelle McGonigle, Richard McLaughlin, David Paquette, Ronald Pare, Charlene Parlee, Henry Parlee, Linda Prescott, Pamela Rivard, Edith Sousa, and the Waite families (Joan Dowling, Kathleen Foster, and George Waite Jr.). Several photographs were available courtesy of a previous project detailing the history of the Chelmsford Fire Department. Remaining photographs were available courtesy of the author's connections with the Chelmsford Historical Society, Chelmsford Historical Commission, and Westford Historical Society & Museum.

INTRODUCTION

Farming was a business and way of life in the villages of South and East Chelmsford from the arrival of the first settlers in the 1650s until its gradual decline in the 1900s. The story of how some of these properties made the transition from farming to conservation land, housing developments, and industry is told here alongside vintage photographs. Heart Pond had commercial use as a source of water for cranberry production for over 100 years and for ice until 1930 but is now residential and recreational.

South Chelmsford was reduced to its present size when the land west of Heart Pond became Westford in 1729, and 17 farms in the south became a district of Carlisle in 1780 and a part of that town in 1805. Families listed on the 1856 Walling's map were Adams, Barton, Battles, Bean, Byam, Dudley, Fiske, Harwood, Hodgman, Lowell, Proctor, Parker, Richardson, Robbins, Spalding, Wilkins, and Wright. Although a significant portion of farmland was sold for housing development in the second half of the 1900s, some of South Chelmsford's rural character remains with restored farmhouses, a few operating farms, and conservation land.

East Chelmsford lost more than half its land in the north to Lowell in 1826. Families listed on the 1856 Walling's map were Atwood, Brown, Dyer, Edmunds, French, Guild, Manning, Marshall, Merriam, Pierce, Spaulding, Wilkins, and Wyman. Farmland was purchased by immigrant families from Canada, Ireland, and Portugal in the late 1800s and early 1900s, with some of that becoming housing subdivisions as Chelmsford rapidly expanded in the late 1900s. Tracts of farmland were also developed for commercial and industrial purposes in the State Route 3 corridor after its construction in the 1950s.

One
KATE'S CORNER

This postcard view of South Chelmsford shows how rural the area was surrounding the cluster of homes and businesses in the village center. The store at 1 Common Street second from right dates the card to after 1909. Houses at 3 Parkerville and 30 Maple Roads are at upper left, the First Baptist Church steeple is at center, and 1 and 5 Common Street are at right. (Chelmsford Historical Society.)

The store at the corner of Maple and Acton roads existed around 1824, when John Bateman and Ezekiel Byam purchased the property from the estate of Peter Proctor. Henry Emerson and later son John owned the store seen here from 1890 to 1922 and combined with Daniel Bickford's store across the street, operated as Emerson & Co. They sold groceries, hardware, coal, fertilizers, feed, and agricultural implements. (Chelmsford Historical Society.)

Emile Paignon from 66 Proctor Road purchased the store from the estate of Henry Emerson in 1922. He also ran a farm supply and grain store at the decommissioned train station nearby and established the South Chelmsford post office there when his daughter Mabel was appointed postmaster in 1924. He sold this corner store in 1925 but regained possession in 1926 when the buyer defaulted on the mortgage. (Chelmsford Historical Society.)

Charles Simpson Jr. purchased two stores from Emile Paignon in 1937: this one at No. 321 and the other across the street at No. 320 Acton Road. He and his wife, Doris, lived at the 1 Common Street variety store (on the cover) next door to Liberty Hall. This store at No. 321, known here as Simpson's Market, became the post office in 1939, with Mabel Paignon serving as postmaster. (Chelmsford Historical Society.)

Salesman Howard Lawson purchased the 321 Acton Road store in 1950, opening it as Lawson's Market. He sold it to George Marchand Jr. in 1954, and it is seen here around that year as Marchand's Market with Mobilgas pumps at left and a Hostess delivery truck out front. George sold the store in 1961 to his son Lionel, who sold it within the year to Elmer Burns. (Chelmsford Historical Society.)

Owner Elmer Burns lived at 21 Davis Road, but Philip and Marjorie McCormack ran the store and lived in the apartment above. The store, seen here in December 1973, was known as Phil's Village Market and was a rural station without a postmaster. In 1975, Philip McCormack purchased the building from Elmer Burns but sold it two months later to carpenter Ronald Wetmore and his wife, Patricia. (Chelmsford Historical Commission.)

Ronald Wetmore ran the store as Ron's Village Market until 1983, when William Keohane from North Chelmsford leased the store and ran it as the Convenience Plus. In May 1993, Kathleen Connors took over the lease, and it became known as Kate's Corner. She purchased the store from Ronald Wetmore in December 1998, and it continues as Kate's Corner, as seen in this August 2004 photograph. (Photograph by the author.)

This postcard panorama from around 1921 shows, from left to right, the First Baptist Church parsonage; a barn belonging to the church; Henry Staveley's blacksmith shop; the Staveley house, 313 Acton Road; the Lyman Byam house, 305 Acton Road; the corner of Lyman Byam's store, 1 Common Street; Liberty Hall, 318 Acton Road; and the John B. Emerson store, 320 Acton Road. (Don MacGillivray.)

Henry Staveley, seen here, and his wife, Jean, purchased the shop, garage, and house at 313 Acton Road in 1909. At the time, it was a good location to service horse traffic passing through South Chelmsford and raise their four children, but when the Great Depression hit in 1929, the family rented a house in Fitchburg, and Henry purchased a delicatessen. They sold their Chelmsford house in 1931. (Linda Prescott.)

This is how 313 Acton Road looked in 1941, the year Annabel Hennessey sold the house to James and Roberta Cofran, with no sign of the old Staveley blacksmith shop. In 1954, Roberta and her new husband, Arthur Smith, sold the house to John and Mary Quigley. Locals then knew it as the Quigley house, as it remained in that family for the next 50 years. (Chelmsford Historical Society.)

The 1899 Annual Town Report states, "At the request of George B. B. Wright, Warren Berry and twenty-three others, to see if the town will vote to purchase a stone watering trough for the well at South Chelmsford." The trough, installed in 1900, was later moved for safekeeping across Acton Road to First Baptist Church property between the now empty original parsonage and church barn sites. (Don MacGillivray.)

Lyman Byam purchased a one-third acre lot at 1 Common Street from John Scoboria in 1909 and built this variety store called Byam & Company. Customers could also drop off their laundry for cleaning at the Middlesex Laundry in Lowell or purchase a popular cold remedy. Those in the doorway are unidentified, but the lady on the right was Henry Emerson's wife, Louise, from 330 Acton Road. (Chelmsford Historical Society.)

The 1 Common Street variety store seen here on the left was purchased by Charles Simpson Jr. in 1923. Mabel Paignon stands in front of Liberty Hall in 1924, the year she was commissioned as postmaster. She remained in office until South Chelmsford was discontinued as an independent post office and established as a rural station in 1965, retiring from postal service in 1966. (Chelmsford Historical Society.)

This postcard was sent by Mabel Paignon to staff sergeant George Waite serving in Spokane, Washington, in December 1942. It shows, from left to right, the Waite farm, Liberty Hall, and the former Bickford store, now a house. The service flag on Liberty Hall was displayed to indicate family members in the Armed Forces during a period of hostilities and had a white background, red border, and blue star. (Waite family.)

Daniel Bickford and his family owned this store at 320 Acton Road from 1879 to 1921 and lived upstairs. Henry Emerson operated the store downstairs as Emerson & Co. along with the store he owned across the street at No. 321. Daniel's son Frank Bickford moved to West Chelmsford village in 1904, where he became postmaster and storekeeper, but owned the house at 326 Acton Road until 1920. (Chelmsford Historical Society.)

The buildings behind the two-horse carriage on Acton Road are, from left to right, Liberty Hall, No. 318; Emerson & Company, No. 320; Frank Bickford, No. 326; and Henry Emerson, No. 330. Henry's son, John, standing in front of No. 330, purchased the store at No. 320 from Floyd Bickford in 1921 but sold it two years later to Emile Paignon. The men in the carriage are not identified. (Chelmsford Historical Commission.)

Charles Simpson Jr., who lived in the 1 Common Street variety store he purchased from Lyman Byam in 1923, purchased the remaining stores at No. 320 and No. 321 from Emile Paignon in 1937. Sometime before 1942, he converted the store at No. 320 into a house, as seen here for his own residence. He added Mobilgas pumps outside the store, and postmaster Mabel Paignon ran the post office inside. (Chelmsford Historical Society.)

Three of five Emerson brothers, Burt, Henry, and James, are standing outside Henry's 330 Acton Road home around 1918. All five brothers, aged 19 to 31, enlisted in various infantry regiments at the beginning of the Civil War and all returned safely, except Henry, who was disabled after 11 months. James's son Ralph Waldo was postmaster in Chelmsford Center, while Henry was postmaster in South Chelmsford. (Chelmsford Historical Society.)

Postmaster Henry Harrison Emerson, seen here next to No. 330, had a cousin Henry Herbert Emerson in Chelmsford the same age who went by Herbert to avoid confusion. The barn at left on the other side of Acton Road and behind the church was built for grain storage by Thomas Gerrish, who owned the store at No. 321 from 1870 to 1890. The barn was removed sometime around 1920. (Chelmsford Historical Society.)

Two

Heart Pond

This is a 1987 aerial view of Heart Pond showing Greenwood Stables in Westford at upper left and Byam's Grove projecting into the pond giving its heart shape. Kate's Corner is at lower left with the Lockheed Martin plant and Agway (Maxwell's) at center. The fields behind Red Wing Farm, now town conservation land, are at lower right, and the edge of the Byam Schoolyard is at far right. (Joan Crandall.)

The Lowell Ice Company purchased land on Heart Pond with an existing icehouse from Hannah Byam in 1896, and when they defaulted on a mortgage two years later, ice and firewood magnate Daniel Gage took control. Hannah's great-granddaughter Rachel Byam is standing on the point of land at the end of Byam's Grove in September 1917, with the icehouse and conveyor at left and railroad tracks at right. (Chelmsford Historical Society.)

On a hot July day in 1924, a large group is enjoying the cool waters of the pond by the front end of the Gage conveyor system. The guide rakes are raised out of the water along with the two chains and crossbars that make up the conveyor belt. Byam's Grove, where Lyman Byam rented campsites and rowboats in the summer, is in the left background. (Chelmsford Historical Society.)

Once ice reached a thickness of 11 inches, crews were hired. Horses with spiked shoes pulled eight-blade "ice plows," as seen above, to cut grooves about three inches deep, forming a grid of rectangular blocks. Rafts of blocks were split off with iron bars and poled toward an open channel where they were split into individual blocks and moved into the conveyor system. The railroad is at right. (Don MacGillivray.)

This crew poled individual blocks into the conveyor system while other crews packed the blocks into five ice houses using marsh grass and sawdust as insulation. The conveyor system ran on steam power from the engine house seen at far left. Ice was shipped year-round on a railroad siding that crossed Pond Street and connected with the main line near the South Chelmsford train station. (Don MacGillivray.)

When Daniel Gage died in 1901, his unmarried daughter Martina Gage took over the company. Sometime after 1917, she expanded the single icehouse on their Heart Pond property to the five storage buildings seen here. In 1929, the Metropolitan Ice Company leased this facility at 28–30 Parkerville Road from Daniel Gage, Inc., but they did not harvest ice in the winters of 1929–1930 or 1930–1931. (Chelmsford Historical Society.)

On a Sunday night, January 1, 1931, fire broke out in the icehouses, and the fire department was alerted by caretaker James Cameron. The icehouse fire was beyond control, but five nearby cottages were saved from the flying sparks. Pond Street is at right, and there is an automobile partially hidden behind one of the birch trees. The beach in the foreground is now the town beach. (Chelmsford Historical Society.)

A series of photographs was taken by postmaster Mabel Paignon around 1932 from a rowboat, and many of those are used in this chapter. This view, looking west from the town beach, includes Lakeside Avenue on the left with the cottages at Nos. 7 and 9 visible at center. The cottage at No. 1 was built in 1933 and is not seen here. A rowboat is pictured at bottom center. (Chelmsford Historical Society.)

Lakeside Avenue was developed starting in 1905 by cranberry growers Warren and James Nickles. In 1929, grocer Charles Simpson Jr. purchased the last lot in the development from the Nickles estate. His summer cottage was built in 1933, typical of the earlier cottages, and nestled in between railroad tracks and the pond. In 2006, the cottage was purchased and later demolished by the Riverside Development Corporation. (Photograph by the author.)

After demolition of the cottage at 1 Lakeside Avenue, the Riverside Development Corporation built a multistory year-round house on the original cottage footprint, as seen here at top center in August 2011. This occasion was a Chelmsford employee and committee party at Heart Pond with pontoon boat rides, kayaks, and a cookout at the town beach. Town manager Paul Cohen is paddling out in the kayak. (Photograph by the author.)

From left to right, around 1932, the Nos. 5, 7, and 9 Lakeside Avenue cottages were part of the Nickles cranberry family subdivision. Charles and Hannah Anderson owned No. 5 until 1949, Edna MacIsaac owned No. 7 until 1953, and Eugene and Celia Gordon (relatives of the author) owned No. 9 until 1954. Large screened porches provided shade, protection from mosquitoes, and sleeping space on hot nights. Wooden rowboats were popular. (Chelmsford Historical Society.)

This view, looking east around 1932, shows, from left to right, Nos. 9, 11, and 12 Lakeside Avenue. The cottages at Nos. 11 and 12 were owned by Addie Nickles, widow of James Nickles of the Nickles Cranberry Company. She sold No. 11 to Harold and Myra Pride in 1933 (until 1953) and No. 12 to Maxwell and Dorothy Carter in 1934 (until 1966). The railroad tracks are at left. (Chelmsford Historical Society.)

This 1907 photograph shows, from left to right, the dam shed, the dam, and 16 Lakeside and 54 Westview Avenues. The dam regulated water flow to the Nickles Cranberry Company bogs in Carlisle for the fall harvest. Nickles sold out to the Lowell Cranberry Company in 1922, and the company sold the land to the Town of Carlisle in 1986. Carlisle Cranberries, Inc. leased the bogs and water rights until 2017. (Pamela Rivard.)

Around 1932, the canal entrance and dam are in between the sailboat in front of 14 Lakeside Avenue and the motorboat in front of 16 Lakeside Avenue. The outboard motor on the mahogany powerboat was most likely a 25-horsepower Evinrude Speed Twin, available since 1929, with a cover over it. This was the only powerboat seen anywhere on the pond. Laundry hangs at 54 Westview Avenue. (Chelmsford Historical Society.)

Addie Nickles sold 16 Lakeside Avenue on the left to Lucy Anderson in 1934 (until 1941 when she sold but retained lifetime use). Grace McGuire owned all of Westview Avenue, including No. 54 on the right, which she inherited from her father Wyman O'Farrell, who purchased it from heirs of Ezekiel Byam in 1901. She leased sites for the building of cottages but retained land ownership until 1961. (Chelmsford Historical Society.)

The cottages left to right are Nos. 54 and 52 Westview Avenue on land owned by Grace McGuire. Frank Saddler was leasing No. 54, and Raymond Elliot was leasing No. 52 (identified here as Candelita) when the land became available for purchase in 1961. Stone retaining walls were built along the shoreline to prevent erosion from storm-generated wave action, especially where cottages were built near the waterline. (Chelmsford Historical Society.)

When land under 46 Westview Avenue, standing out on the right, became available in 1961, it was purchased by lessees Earl and Hazel Norse. Currently, the home is occupied by singer Sandra Spence and her husband, Paul Goulet. Hidden behind trees at far right, 44 Westview Avenue was purchased in 1961 by lessees Mae and Elmer Forslind. The outboard motorboat is moored in the water at left. (Chelmsford Historical Society.)

The cottages at Nos. 46, 44, and 42 Westview Avenue were all built on land owned by Grace McGuire. Lessees George and Grace Carr purchased their land at 42 Westview Avenue in 1961 but sold the property in 1962. It appears the end of the summer season is near as some windows are covered up, and there is no sign of lawn chairs or hanging laundry. (Chelmsford Historical Society.)

Cottages from left to right are at Nos. 44, 42, 40, and 38 Westview Avenue. Lessees Harry and Marion Ledgard purchased their 40 Westview Avenue land in 1961 (until 1986). Lessees Knut and Doris Magnusson purchased the land at 38 Westview Avenue, hidden in the trees (until 1977). A Westview Association was formed to arrange for services such as snow plowing and general betterment of the neighborhood. (Chelmsford Historical Society.)

Lessee Joseph Chaput purchased the land at No. 32, behind and left of No. 28 on the high ground, in 1961 and sold to the Gregoire-Whitney family in 1967 (until 2014). The land at No. 28 was purchased in 1961 by lessees Raymond and Doris Hurley, who kept the home in the family until 1988, when they sold to Martha, Luce, and Virginia Robinson. (Chelmsford Historical Society.)

Lessee Florence Puffer purchased the land at 24 Westview Avenue, on the right high up on the embankment, in 1961, along with three other lots within the subdivision plan. This was inherited by Raymond Hurley, who had purchased two other adjacent lots in 1961. The property was sold to George Kacek in 1975. Kacek organized the Westview Association and served on it until his death in 2018. (Chelmsford Historical Society.)

Land at 14 Westview Avenue was purchased by lessees Ishobel and Andrew Glover along with two other lots in the subdivision. It remained in the family until sold to Amba and writer Robert Coltman in 1974. The man next to the sailboat in the 1930s one-piece wool swimsuit might be dragging a submersible fish cage used to hold live catch until it was time for dinner. (Chelmsford Historical Society.)

The land at 4 Westview Avenue was purchased by lessee Eva Dobson with an additional lot in 1961. Two years later, she sold the camp, and there were several owners until 1996, when it was purchased by Ruth and Herb Marcus. The Marcuses were accomplished ocean-going sailors and served on the board of the Hart Pond Association, dedicated to the health and safety of the pond. (Chelmsford Historical Society.)

Lots 1 through 4 of Grace McGuire's subdivision were combined to form 2 Westview Avenue in 1961 and purchased by lessees Charles and Bertha Sigerson. In 1964, they sold this camp and large lot to Dr. David and Harriet Latham, who remained until 1982. Dominic and Janet Altobello purchased the property in 1988, and it remains in that family. (Chelmsford Historical Society.)

This is the view from 2 Westview Avenue around 1932. Second through Seventh Lanes are directly across the pond, and to the left is one of two inlets that feed into the pond. Accessible only by kayak or canoe, the inlets are habitat for ducks, geese, turtles (both snappers and painted), great blue heron, a variety of birds of prey, and beaver. (Chelmsford Historical Society.)

This Daniel Gage Co. icehouse, seen here around 1907, was located in between today's Westview and Northview Avenues on one-and-a-half acres of land leased from Henry McGuire (Grace McGuire's husband). In 1929, Metropolitan Ice Company from Somerville, Massachusetts, leased the operation for 10 years with the restriction that "ice cannot be shipped to Lowell or surrounding towns without written consent of Henry McGuire." They surrendered this lease in 1936 and, sometime afterward, purchased the land. In 1943, Metropolitan Ice sold 14 acres of land surrounding the icehouse complex to the towns of Chelmsford and Westford and sold the icehouse and five other parcels of land to Fredrick Pond. Gage Road in Westford was the only access route to the icehouse, and the Chelmsford end of that road is now the Northview Avenue waterfront community. (Both, Westford Historical Society & Museum.)

This is the view looking west from First Lane. The raft at left was put out each summer by Lyman Byam's family. His youngest son, Arthur, related that their raft had hooks underneath for bathing suits to be temporarily hung for nighttime swimming (or skinny-dipping). Pond residents often rowed their boats around the distant point to the 4-H fairground during events, thus avoiding the entry fee. (Chelmsford Historical Society.)

This is a view of Lapham's Grove with 26 Fifth Lane (two separate cottages in 1932) on the left and 26 Fourth Lane at center. Eldad Bean paid $300 for five acres of land at the Joseph Chamberlain estate auction in 1865, and this was later passed down to Eldad's grandsons Wilbur and Edgar Lapham. There were facilities here for swimming, picnicking, and boating. (Chelmsford Historical Society.)

In 1932, these cottages were owned by Wilbur and Edgar Lapham. They sold both in 1941. In 1951 and 1952, Ernest Kimball purchased both properties and joined them together to make one dwelling with an address of 26 Fifth Lane. The right-hand cottage now houses an indoor pool, the addition in between is a large kitchen area, and the left-hand cottage is living space. (Chelmsford Historical Society.)

Lapham's Grove, with rowboats in the foreground, consisted of several parcels. Wilbur Lapham purchased 54 Second Lane and 20 Fourth Lane from Frank Byam in 1916. Brothers Edgar and Wilbur Lapham inherited 26 Fourth Lane and Nos. 26, 30, 32, and 40 Fifth Lane from maternal grandfather Eldad Bean. Although all but 32 Fifth Lane were sold out of the family by 1947, the Lapham Lake Association still exists. (Chelmsford Historical Society.)

This photograph captures the west side of the peninsula called Byam's Grove on First Lane around 1932. The Lyman Byam cottage at No. 50 is seen here on the high point of the land. Prime swimming area on the property was directly in front of that cottage. The sandy embankments were subject to erosion, and in later years trees and shrubs were encouraged to grow there. (Chelmsford Historical Society.)

The Lyman Byam family is lined up by height beside their cottage on First Lane in October 1915. From left to right are Amy, Rachel, Lyman Jr., Kenneth, Viola, Evelyn, Grace (shortly to give birth to her ninth child, Frank), and Lyman. Oldest son Edwin took the photograph. The campground store is on the left, and two chicken coops behind the store were later joined to make a bungalow. (Pamela Rivard.)

The occasion for this family photograph is Grace Byam's 42nd birthday on June 16, 1918. Grace is seated at center in a chair specially decorated by the children. From left to right are (first row, seated) Amy (on Lyman's lap), Rachel, Grace (holding baby Arthur), Edwin (holding Frank); (second row, standing) Lyman Jr., Viola, Evelyn, and Kenneth. The family's bungalow is at left. (Pamela Rivard.)

Twenty-year-old Edwin Byam is bailing out one of six wooden rental rowboats in June 1918. These boats required scraping, caulking, and repainting every spring and were part of the campground his father Lyman ran called Byam's Grove. He also maintained a small store to supply campers and day picnickers with essentials for an enjoyable day on the pond. Lakeside Avenue can be seen in the distance. (Pamela Rivard.)

This five-room cottage was built by Lyman Byam in 1901 on First Lane and is seen here in 1918. Known within the family simply as "Camp," it was one of the first cottages on the pond. Nine Byams are on the porch. From left to right are (first row) Frank, Rachel, Amy, and Lyman Jr. (perched on the wall); (second row) Grace, Evelyn, Viola, and Kenneth. (Pamela Rivard.)

Nightly gatherings at the Byam cottage sometimes included stories and hymns and popcorn cooked over the woodstove. Seen here around 1949, family members are, from left to right, Stella Byam, Amy (Byam) Volk, Nicholas Byam, Florence Byam, Grace Byam, Arthur Byam's wife Roberta, and Rachel (Byam) Meyer, who lived to age 104. All nine of Grace and Lyman's living children reunited at First Lane yearly until 1979, when Grace died. (Pamela Rivard.)

Lyman and Grace Byam are sitting in front of their bungalow around 1949. Built by Lyman on First Lane for summer visitors, it consisted of two chicken coops joined together with an added screen porch. It had an indoor hand pump for water and an outhouse nearby. Although Lyman lived a good long life to age 85, Grace outlived him by many years, dying at age 103 in 1979. (Pamela Rivard.)

Grace Byam stands on the pond side of the First Lane cottage with her beloved dog Duke around 1952. The wrap-around porch had heavy shutters that were lowered to cover the screened openings during summer storms and in winter to secure the cottage until the family returned in the spring. When not at camp, the family lived in their South Chelmsford home at 305 Acton Road. (Pamela Rivard.)

Lyman Byam's son Frank built this cottage at 49 First Lane in 1950 at a cost of $5,000. Frank was the only of Lyman's children to build on the Byam's Grove land. These casement windows were installed to catch the breezes. Frank's daughter Pamela and her husband, Norman "Bud" Rivard, demolished this cottage in 2004 to build a year-round home they named Hearts' Desire. (Pamela Rivard.)

Frank's cottage on First Lane measured 24 by 28 feet, and the porch area shown here was used as the master bedroom, with windows looking out at the pond. There was another bedroom inside the cottage for the children as well as an extra bed at the other end of this porch. First Lane Byam cottages were furnished with family hand-me-downs but with nothing deemed "too good for Camp." (Pamela Rivard.)

The living room, in 1952, had this bed that doubled as a sofa, a black-and-white TV, and a ladder-access loft above that served as storage and a child's play area. A comfortable chair and reading lamp were out of view, and the dining area and kitchen were at the other end. The floor covering was linoleum, and the interior walls were designed to be movable. (Pamela Rivard.)

Cold water for this kitchen and a half bath was pumped from a perforated pointed pipe pounded into the ground in the side yard. Hot water heated in the large kettle on the stove was used for washing dishes and sponge baths. With only a half bath inside, the family bathed in the pond until 1975, when son-in-law Norman Rivard installed an outdoor shower and hot water heater. (Pamela Rivard.)

Three

FARMING LIFE

This aerial view of South Chelmsford shows active farmland in 1987. The Waite Farm at lower left now supports a horse stable and riding operation. Jones Farm leased land at the bottom center for a greenhouse and community composting. The Lewis Farm at lower right became Sunny Meadow Farm community garden and a guest farmer collaborative. Byam farmlands at the middle center are now part of Red Wing Farm. (Joan Crandall.)

There were four George Wrights in early-1900s Chelmsford. George C. was a minister in Lowell, George M. was a blacksmith in Central Square, and George S. was a superintendent of Chelmsford schools. George B.B. Wright, who grew up with his parents, Calvin and Martha, at 200 Action Road, was a nurseryman and lived in this 187 Acton Road home he and his wife, Adelaide, purchased in 1893. (Chelmsford Historical Society.)

Nurseryman George Wright had a horse and a few cows on his farm in support of the family, but his main business was the nursery, advertising "decorative shrubs and vines, small fruits, grape vines, rose bushes, herbaceous plants, etc." Here, he is riding in the orchard on a single-axle cart, which was the equivalent of a pickup truck in its day. George and Adelaide had two daughters. (Chelmsford Historical Society.)

In 1912 and 1913, George purchased four parcels of land totaling about 31 acres on the other side of Acton Road to expand the nursery business. His daughters Ethel and Adelaide pick pansies in the new planting beds in 1913. A nursery building at right was constructed up against the stone retaining wall on Acton Road, and a ladder stands where a stairway was later constructed. (Chelmsford Historical Society.)

George stands among young trees next to the nursery building in 1914, with the completed set of stairs on the left. The Robin Hill Nursery, as it was now called, was the only landscaping business listed in the town directory, and a crew of laborers was hired to work in the yard and on customers' landscaping projects. His daughter Adelaide taught in Marblehead this year. (Chelmsford Historical Society.)

This landscaping crew has a load of trees and shrubs ready to deliver in 1915 in an early chain-drive stake-bed truck. This was a step up from a horse-drawn wagon but has the obvious disadvantages of solid rubber tires, a vulnerable pair of chains, and little protection from the weather. The men in the photograph were not identified, but the sign speaks for itself. (Chelmsford Historical Society.)

Herbert Whiting, a cranberry grower from Plymouth and relative of George's wife, Adelaide, had a son named Benjamin in 1913. Herbert's wife died in 1916, and he remarried a year later. Benjamin was sent to Chelmsford and became a part of the Wright household for several years, attending school and helping with the nursery business. Benjamin poses with his Kodak Brownie box camera in 1924. (Chelmsford Historical Society.)

Napoleon and Rosalie Manseau from Canada raised 10 children at 14 Parker Road, and their son Gedeon became a valued worker at the Robin Hill Nursery. Benjamin and Gedeon are chopping firewood here, a regular chore on farms heated with wood from a nearby woodlot. Ethel Wright's diary mentions Gedeon frequently as he ran all sorts of errands, including driving the car as the family chauffeur. (Chelmsford Historical Society.)

George pitches the second crop of hay onto a one-horse hay wagon in 1924, with Gedeon on top, packing down the load. The nursery product line now included "Shade and ornamental trees, choice evergreens and box trees, heavy evergreen, fruit stock etc., hardy perennials, shrubbery of all kinds." Daughter Adelaide was still teaching in Marblehead and, in later years, became a librarian at the Adams Library. (Chelmsford Historical Society.)

The nursery had a stone loading dock on Acton Road, making it convenient to drag trees by horse up the ramp and roll them into the latest stake-bed delivery truck. From left to right, in 1924, George, Gedeon, and Ben check a load of trees destined for Crocker Athletic Field in Fitchburg, Massachusetts, designed by the sons of Frederic Law Olmsted and dedicated in 1918. (Chelmsford Historical Society.)

George Wright died in 1926, and his daughter Ethel became the manager of Robin Hill Nursery, with Gedeon Manseau as foreman. By 1937, Gedeon and neighbor John Fay were the nurserymen, and Gedeon moved into 187 Acton Road. He married Laurette Cossette in 1940 and died in 1979, but Laurette remained at 187 Acton Road until 1987, when the house was sold by heirs of the Wright family. (Chelmsford Historical Society.)

This 1924 photograph is a rare view of the working farm at 40 Byam Road. The silo and chicken houses were later removed, and the barn cut in half. Donated by the Murray family in 1969, it is now the home of the Chelmsford Historical Society. The George Wright fields in the foreground are now Brush Hill Road, and the 1918 steel fire tower is above right. (Chelmsford Historical Society.)

Lester Ball was the forest fire observer in the temporary wooden tower built on Robins Hill after the 1938 hurricane destroyed the steel tower. His wife, Adelaide, Ethel Wright's sister, inherited Robin Hill Nursery and 187 Acton Road when Ethel died in 1948. The next year, Lester and Adelaide sold their house at 170 Acton Road and moved into No. 187 with Gedeon Manseau running the nursery. (Chelmsford Historical Society.)

Benjamin Chamberlain operated the former Manning tavern at 109 Billerica Road next to the Middlesex Turnpike. He liked the design of that house, so when his daughter Martha married Calvin Wright in 1842, he built this similar house for her at 200 Acton Road. Calvin sold the property to his father-in-law, Benjamin, in 1851, but the Wright family continued to live in the house. (Chelmsford Historical Society.)

Benjamin died, and in 1893 his widow, Asenath (Manning) Chamberlain, sold the house to Calvin Wright's children, Caroline, Adelia, George, Juliette, and Edward, subject to a life tenancy for their father, Calvin. Caroline, Adelia, and George were married and living elsewhere, so by 1901, they sold their interests in the farm to unmarried siblings Edward and Juliette. (Chelmsford Historical Society.)

Edward Wright is seen driving his two-horse dump cart around 1921, with farmhand Harvey Cann and his son Frederick in the rear. The extra-large rear wheels supported a heavy load balanced over the rear axle so it could be tilted back with minimum effort. The bench seat was cushioned for the driver's comfort. Edward was a farmer and milk dealer before his death in 1932. (Chelmsford Historical Society.)

A small house attached to the rear of the barn was used by George Wright before moving across the street to 187 Acton Road and later served as an apartment for hired hands. Farm laborer Harvey Cann and his wife, Norah, were originally at Central House but moved into the apartment in the mid-1920s with their three children. Norah is in the barn with her cat. (Chelmsford Historical Society.)

Juliette and Ethel Wright, trustee for Edward Wright's estate, sold the farm to Edward Alcorn in 1936. Edward lived on his parent's farm at 150 Hunt Road, next to the present Alcorn Road, and rented out 200 Acton Road for five years. In 1944, he sold the farm to his married older brother Walter, who had returned to Chelmsford and was living at 11 Davis Road. (Chelmsford Historical Society.)

Walter and his wife, Mary, raised turkeys and ran a farm stand at 200 Acton Road. Walter died in July 1968, and in September, Campanelli, Inc. of Braintree, Massachusetts, purchased Mary's farm, seen here, and adjacent land owned by the heirs of Alfred Paasche. A 73-lot Hickory Hills development was surveyed with Burning Tree Lane, Drew Circle, and DeWolfe, Green Valley, Country Club, and Smoke Rise Drives. (Chelmsford Historical Society.)

The National Environmental Protection Act was signed in 1970, and by 1972 the Chelmsford Conservation Commission was beginning to exercise its state mandate to inventory and protect wetlands. Twenty-two of the lots on Green Valley Drive were in wetlands, and in December 1972 Campanelli decided to transfer ownership to the town for $1. This new conservation land connects with the George B.B. Wright Reservation. (Photograph by the author.)

The farm at 246 Acton Road was operated by the Dupee family since 1860, primarily as an apple orchard, and after the 1938 hurricane, as a dairy. Sidney Dupee was the last generation, hiring farmhands Alfred House, and later, his younger brother Ralph, from 330 Acton Road. Ralph House became the farm manager in 1942 at age 25, and in 1956 he purchased the 36-acre farm from Sidney. (Deborah Jones.)

The pyramidal building at right in this July 1939 photograph was originally the base of a windmill used for apple processing and was moved here as a milk room. Ralph House Construction set up headquarters here at 246 Acton Road. This and nearby parcels Ralph purchased from 1952 to 1962 were developed into Greenacre Lane, Jerridge Lane, Kenwood Street, Linden Street, and 13 lots on Park Road. (Deborah Jones.)

By the time farmer Philip Jones purchased 246 Acton Road in January 1988, there were only four acres left, and the large barn had been demolished. He is seen here in October 2006, with his garden center decorated for Halloween. Philip, a regular contributor to farmers' markets, leased farmland at Sunny Meadow Farm on the other side of Acton Road and at 79 Elm Street. (Photograph by the author.)

Daniel Byam is standing in the doorway of his blacksmith shop at 7 Maple Road in 1908. His father, Marcus, purchased the land from brother-in-law Parker Chamberlain in 1832, under the condition he build a blacksmith shop within three years. Daniel manufactured sleds in the shop until he died in 1918. The shop was moved to the Old Garrison House Association grounds in 1977, where it is on display. (Linda Prescott.)

In 1834, Marcus Byam purchased a half-acre lot at 11 Maple Road from Parker Chamberlain, and by 1840, had his house and barn constructed. Marcus and then Daniel farmed the land across the street and next door to the First Baptist Church, as seen here. In 1953, developer Ralph House purchased this land and, with Bradford Emerson, in 1974, sold it to Frequency Sources Inc. (Chelmsford Historical Society.)

This panoramic photograph, taken around 1880, shows, from left to right, 19 Maple Road, Robins Hill before the Summit House was constructed, 11 Maple Road, the First Baptist Church, the Thomas Gerrish grain barn, and Acton Road in the foreground. The farm at 19 Maple Road was built in the 1730s by Richard Hildreth, about 100 years before 11 Maple Road. Solomon Byam, brother of Marcus, purchased 19 Maple Road from his unmarried brother-in-law Thomas Adams

in 1847. Thomas stayed on with Solomon, and together, they produced Indian corn, potatoes, vegetables, and hay for their dairy cows. From 1850 until 1873, they increased dairy production, especially butter, to serve a regional market. The Baptist Society was formed in 1771, the present church was built in 1836, and the horse sheds were torn down after damage from the 1938 hurricane. (Don MacGillivray.)

Daniel Byam, a Civil War veteran, wrote letters home from 1864 to 1865 and described surviving a train rollover near Valley Forge. He died in 1918, and the 11 Maple Road farm, seen here in 1972, was passed to daughter Ednah, daughter Alta, Ednah's daughter Eleanor Parkhurst, and finally, Alta's stepdaughter and quilter Sally Field. She sold the farm out of the family to Charles and Jeanne Parlee in 2011. (Chelmsford Historical Commission.)

Frank Byam inherited the 19 Maple Road farm when his father, Solomon, died in 1873. He continued to operate the farm, adding apple orchards and poultry and egg production but dropping the sale of butter. In this photograph, Frank gathers hay for his dairy cows on his cousin Daniel's land across Maple Road. He was very active in town affairs and the First Baptist Church, seen at right. (Pamela Rivard.)

This photograph shows the extensive Frank Byam farm complex around 1910. The sign on the barn reads, "Worcester Buckets and Implements." The long ell between house and barns contained the kitchen and carriage house and extended behind the house to provide more living space. The horse and dairy barns are at right. In 1934, one year after Frank died, heirs sold the farm out of the family. (Kevin Cantrell.)

After 1938, the barns were gradually eliminated as needs changed, and maintenance became excessive. Richard and Constance Porter, the owners in 1957, made use of the old dairy barn for horses, as seen here. The Porters gave the property the name "Red Wing Farm," as posted on the tree. The railroad tracks ran between 19 Maple Road and the house at 23 Maple Road, seen at left. (Chelmsford Historical Society.)

Nancy Bartleson became the owner of Red Wing Farm in 2000 when her husband died. Two years later, the town purchased the property and divided it into two parcels, with 1.32 acres to remain with the house and 12.6 acres to remain as conservation land with public access and trails. This officially named Hildreth-Robbins House was placed in the National Register of Historic Places in 2005. (Photograph by the author.)

This 1962 aerial view shows the Lewis farm with the house on Robin Hill Road on the left and barn complex at center. The three-story barn had calves, sheep, chickens, and hay storage upstairs and dairy cows on the ground level and in the one-story extension at right. The building in the foreground housed milk processing and farm equipment. Corn from the field above was chopped for silage. (Joan Crandall.)

Walter and Bessie Lewis purchased the farm at 172 Robin Hill Road in 1942 from heirs of the Lapham family, who acquired the land as a pre-Revolutionary grant from the King of England. Seen here in 1952, from left to right, are (first row) Joan Lewis and a family friend holding one of Walter's specially bred hens; (second row) Nancy, Bessie, Richard, and Walter Lewis. (Joan Crandall.)

When starting up the dairy, a few weeks of milking cows by hand quickly convinced Walter to purchase a milking machine system, as seen here. The DeJesus Dairy in East Chelmsford pasteurized and bottled his milk. When homogenization also became a requirement, he switched to Andrew Boumil's Suburban Dairy at 60 Richardson Road. Suburban Dairy collected milk from area farms with a one-and-a-half-ton bulk milk truck. (Joan Crandall.)

Walter and son Richard are in the chicken coop on an upper floor of the barn. The A&P Company ran a contest in 1948 to see if anyone could breed a better chicken for sale in their supermarkets. Walter and brother-in-law Ellery Metcalf entered the contest and won with a new breed called "White American" for its feather coloring. Walter raised this breed to sell as poultry. (Joan Crandall.)

Canning to preserve crops for year-round eating was a part of life on the farm. It was first invented by French chemist Nicolas Appert in response to a large prize offered by Napoleon to anyone who could figure out a way to preserve food for his troops. Nancy and Bessie Lewis are showing *Lowell Sun* photographer Joseph Principato some of the food stored in their basement in 1952. (Joan Crandall.)

Walter is seen here greasing the manure spreader while farmhand Thomas Taylor is cleaning the inside, and son Richard Lewis is sitting on the tractor. Walter attended Essex Agricultural School in Danvers, received a bachelor's degree in poultry from the University of Massachusetts, and a master's degree in agricultural economics from the University of Connecticut. He then worked two years at the University of New Hampshire before buying the farm in Chelmsford. (Joan Crandall.)

Chopped corn for winter feed was stored in a trench silo cut into the ground near the barn. This solved two problems associated with the use of the vertical silo: maintenance and storage of a conveyor belt system to load the silo and ventilation of nitric oxide gas that could produce toxic byproducts during the fermentation process. Farmworkers John Gravelle and Thomas Taylor are loading the truck. (Joan Crandall.)

In 1968, Walter purchased his own pasteurizing, homogenizing, and bottling equipment. This was installed in a separate building that was an expanded farm equipment garage. The name "Sunny Meadow Farm" used on these milk bottles and other products originated from a comment made by son Richard Lewis when looking out over the meadows on a sunny day. This production operator was Rasburan Bryan from Lowell. (Joan Crandall.)

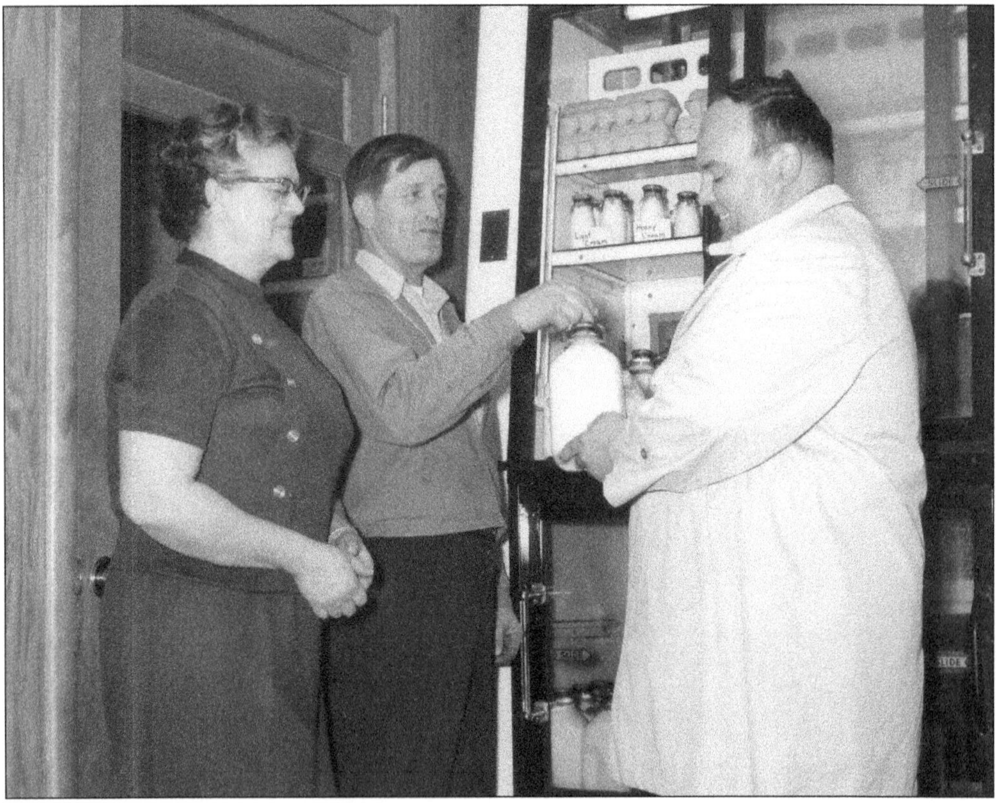

Bessie and Walter operated a small farm store in the milk-processing building for the sale of poultry and dairy products, as seen here with an unidentified customer. Walter grew up in Andover near today's Internal Revenue Service building and delivered unpasteurized raw milk daily from the family farm. He could have legally sold raw milk in his Chelmsford store but chose not to take the risk. (Joan Crandall.)

On December 5, 1970, Walter was flying to an American Farm Bureau Federation meeting in Houston, Texas, when a fire broke out in the main barn hayloft around 4:30 p.m. Grandson Daniel Lewis inside the house first noticed the fire and ran outside. Three outside workers and two men milking the cows inside acted quickly to lead about 85 cows and a calf to safety in a field. (Chelmsford Fire Department.)

Fifteen fire trucks from four communities responded to the alarm and brought the blaze under control after a two-hour battle. The fire was stopped at the milk room connecting the barn to the house, and the winter feed in the outdoor pit was saved, but several calves and two sheep perished. After the fire, Walter and Bessie moved next door to 182 Robin Hill Road. (Joan Crandall.)

The cows were initially transported to a farm in Concord, Massachusetts, and Walter formed a partnership with the farm owner, bottling and distributing their milk. The partnership was dissolved after two years, but Walter continued processing the milk in his own plant and delivering with his trucks. He finally gave up that business in July 1976 and auctioned off the dairy and delivery equipment in August that year. (Joan Crandall.)

A garage was added to the original 172 Robin Hill Road farmhouse at left. After the milk-processing equipment and store were removed from the building at center, Walter converted that space into an apartment with address 174 Robin Hill Road. A two-car garage was built on the foundation of the dairy barn extension at right, and Walter later added another apartment with address 170 Robin Hill Road. (Joan Crandall.)

In 1978, Walter and Bessie moved back home to 172 Robin Hill Road. This August 1987 aerial view shows houses, from left to right, Nos. 182, 174, 170, and 172 Robin Hill Road. Walter set up a horse farm on the right with a new barn, paddocks, and a track for jumping. He and his daughter Joan partnered in Sunny Meadow Homes, rehabilitating or constructing several houses a year. (Joan Crandall.)

Cambodian refugee Sum Chey was invited to set up a garden on unused Lewis land in 1985, and by 1989, he was supplying Asian markets in Lowell, Boston, and Providence. The Town of Chelmsford purchased the Lewis farmland in June 2008, and the Walter F. Lewis Community Garden was dedicated, as seen here on August 15, 2009. The Chey family greenhouses are in the background. (Photograph by the author.)

In 1924, Samuel and Margaret Parlee purchased this house with 18 acres at 135 Pine Hill Road. Samuel was a carpenter and 1 of 10 children of Concord Road farmer William Parlee. Samuel died in 1936 at only 45 years old, predeceasing his father, William, but his family of six boys prospered. The house passed to Samuel's son Ralph and then to Ralph's nephew Henry Jr. and his family. (Henry Parlee.)

The Parlee sons are behind 135 Pine Hill Road around 1940. From left to right are Charles, Robert, mother Margaret, Henry, Ralph, Edward, and Frederick. Charles became a commercial developer and farmer, Robert had an Air Force career in Louisiana, Henry owned Parlee Lumber in Littleton, Massachusetts, Ralph became a poultry and produce farmer, Edward worked at Merrimack Mills then Raytheon, and Frederick was a machinist at GE in Lynn. (Henry Parlee.)

This aerial view shows the Charles Parlee field at lower left, later leased by Weston Nurseries Garden Center, and the old Dutton house that Charles restored at the intersection of Hunt and Pine Hill Roads at bottom center. The Ralph Parlee farmlands are at center, and between 1952 and 1993 Ralph added six parcels of farmland and several barns to the original Samuel Parlee homestead. (Henry Parlee.)

In the 1950s, Ralph worked as a corduroy cutter to supplement his income while building a large chicken coop, establishing strawberry beds, and preparing fields for other crops. As business grew, he purchased more farmland nearby and leased land from the Sheehan family at the intersection of Galloway and Pine Hill Roads and from the Lewis family at both Robin Hill and Garrison Roads. (Henry Parlee.)

The pick-your-own strawberry business peaked in the 1970s, and this was a very busy day in the field down behind the house. On every frost warning, family and friends were enlisted to man pumps and spray water onto all the plants to form a layer of ice that would protect the plants from freezing. Ponds had to be dug if there was no natural water supply nearby. (Henry Parlee.)

Henry Parlee Jr. lived next door at 125 Pine Hill Road and worked on his uncle Ralph's farm. The open shed was originally built for mulch and as shelter for beef cattle the family raised in the late 1970s and early 1980s. The first barn beyond was built by his uncle Frederick for raising brooder hens and was later used for horses with hay on the upper floors. (Henry Parlee.)

Henry is in one of Ralph's strawberry patches with his son Nicholas around 1993. The Parlee name was associated with strawberries even outside Chelmsford. Henry's first cousin Mark, from Tyngsboro, started planting strawberries in 1987, the year his father, Edward, retired from Raytheon, with guidance from uncle Ralph. He built up an impressive 93-acre "Parlee Farm" near the banks of the Merrimack River, growing fruits, vegetables, and flowers. (Henry Parlee.)

In this 1996 photograph, Ralph is seated on his favorite tractor: an easy-to-operate Kubota purchased around 1979. After Ralph's death in August 1999, Henry Jr. inherited the house and farm at 135 Pine Hill Road. Henry continued farming, later joined by his daughter Caroline who sold blueberries, corn, squash, strawberries, and tomatoes at the farm stand on Pine Hill Road to earn money for college expenses. (Henry Parlee.)

This sketch was done in charcoal and wash by artist James Franklin Gilman in 1872. At the time, this 75-acre farm was occupied by Elbridge and Laura Dutton with their sons Edwin and Lewis. After Elbridge's death in 1879, Lewis sold his inherited share of the farm to Edwin. In 1884, they purchased David Perham's Central Square sawmill, gristmill, and icehouse complex as the Dutton Brothers. (Charlene Parlee.)

When Edwin died in 1901, his wife, Carrie, inherited, and soon after she died in 1927 her sons Arthur, Charles, Francis, and Harry Dutton sold their shares of 143 Pine Hill Road to their brother and sister Leroy and Laura Dutton. Leroy ran a small dairy at the farm and is seen here with a pair of calves. He and his wife, Catherine, raised two of her nieces. (Henry Parlee.)

Catherine Dutton's niece Catherine Allen is at lower left, and her sister Eleanor Allen is seen upper right around 1940. Alice McHugh is at upper left, and her brother Warren McHugh is at lower right. Both Alice and Warren became captains of their Chelmsford High School basketball teams. Eight McHugh children grew up in the original farmhouse at what is now 5 McHugh Farm Lane. (Henry Parlee.)

Leroy's brother Arthur from 161 High Street ran market garden and greenhouse businesses across Pine Hill Road until his death in 1951. Much of the Dutton and McHugh farmland was taken in the late 1950s for construction of Interstate 495. Leroy and Catherine died in 1965 and 1967, and when Charles Parlee purchased the farm from Laura in 1974, it was in bad shape, as seen here. (Chelmsford Historical Commission.)

Charles Parlee left school permanently while in the fifth grade to help his mother run the farm when his father died young in 1936. Jeanne (Dumont) and Charles, posing by a vine trellis, were married in 1951. From 1951 until 1959, they lived in a travel trailer set up in the back field until Jeanne got startled by a cow, and they moved it up near the house. (Henry Parlee.)

This is the travel trailer installed near the house at 135 Pine Hill Road. Jeanne's mother, Mary Dumont, was caring for this girl named Rita. In 1957, Charles purchased a house lot at 164 Pine Hill Road from Leroy and Laura Dutton, completed construction in 1959, and moved in. He purchased half interests in land at 160 Pine Hill Road from Laura and Catherine Dutton in 1965. (Henry Parlee.)

Charles and Jeanne Parlee purchased the 143 Pine Hill Road Dutton house from Laura Dutton in 1974. Contractors were hired to restore the house to the configuration shown in the 1872 James Franklin Gilman sketch, then owned by the Dutton family. Charles and Jeanne purchased the sketch in 1977. In this photograph, the ell on the left was removed, and the right rear porches were being demolished. (Chelmsford Historical Society.)

Around 1977, the Charles Parlee family moved into their newly restored 143 Pine Hill Road farm. This photograph shows the house after completion and a crew shingling the barn roof. Starting in the 1950s, Charles had partnered with Jeanne's brother Emile Dumont in the construction of residential and commercial projects starting with Alpine Lane off Route 110. The partnership ended in 1978, with the two splitting assets evenly. (Henry Parlee.)

Alexander Park constructed what was then called "the nicest house in town" at 69 Park Road in 1898 and ran his father's greenhouse and market garden operation on six acres next door. Alexander's untimely death near his 40th birthday in December 1906 forced an auction of the entire property. Augustus Waite from Dunbarton, New Hampshire, purchased the estate at auction in 1908 for less than $6,000. (Chelmsford Historical Society.)

This 4 Proctor Road home was built by Revolutionary War veteran Lt. John Bateman, from Concord, Massachusetts, around 1787. After his death, the estate went to his son-in-law Ezekiel Byam, a trader and match manufacturer who had married Charlotte Bateman in 1818. Ezekiel died in 1862, and the farm was owned by Daniel Raymond in 1872 when this charcoal and pencil sketch was done by artist James Franklin Gilman. (Charlene Parlee.)

Augustus Waite's son George and farmer William Belleville ran "Belleville and Waite, Market Gardeners" at 69 Park Road. In 1920, Augustus sold that farm to William, and in 1923 George purchased another farm at 4 Proctor Road. In 1929, William sold 69 Park Road and moved to New Jersey, and the Augustus and George Waite families moved into 4 Proctor Road, seen here in September 1940. (Chelmsford Historical Society.)

The Waite family is on the front porch at 4 Proctor Road around 1942. From left to right are George L. Waite, daughter Elizabeth Whalen, grandchildren Ann and Louise Whalen, wife Delia, and son George F. Waite. Delia was a sister of business partner William Belleville and aunt of Walter Belleville Jr., a World War II casualty who is remembered with a square in front of 4 Proctor Road. (The Waite family.)

After George L. Waite died in 1948 at age 62, his son and daughter-in-law George F. and Marguerite continued farming. In 1968, an elementary school site search committee was concerned about railroad tracks being close to the available Blaisdell farm site on Maple Road and preferred this field on the Waite farm. George fought the plan, and in 1970 the Blaisdell farm became the site of Byam School. (The Waite family.)

Pictured from left to right, grandchildren Kathryn and Kristen Dowling are in the tomato field. When weatherman Don Kent issued a frost warning, bushel baskets were moved out of the barn and stacked nearby to place over the plants. When the sun went down, it was all-hands-on-deck to cover the plants. Sometimes, customers would see the activity in the field and pull over to help. (The Waite family.)

In late spring, George and Marguerite picked strawberries to order for regular customers and delivered to their homes. George and his brother-in-law John Hallberg were volunteer firefighters with Engine 5 across the street on Acton Road, with George serving as captain in the 1950s. To pay the bills from November to February, George drove an oil delivery truck for Labonte Oil in Tewksbury, later Mahoney Oil in Lowell. (The Waite family.)

In mid-July, after the strawberry crop was finished, the farm stand would open for business, with loyal teen workers wearing pink "Waite Farm" tee shirts. Homemade greenhouses and cold frames were used in March to get an early start on tomatoes and green peppers and then cabbage, broccoli, and cauliflower. Also sold at the stand were yellow and green beans, beets, carrots, cucumbers, corn, onions, summer squash, and zucchini. (The Waite family.)

George Waite leased land on other farms, including the Lewis farm across Acton Road, seen here. The Lewis family house and horse corral are at center and right. Getting on in years, George approached Charles Parlee to see if he was interested in purchasing the farm. The sale and mortgage were finalized in November 1987, and proceeds were shared with George's sisters Elisabeth Whalen and Lois Hallberg. (The Waite family.)

With an open invitation to continue farming at 4 Proctor Road, George Jr. raised pumpkins as seen here around 1989. George and Marguerite needed a new place to live, and daughter Kathleen had recently moved out of her home at 223 Park Road near the Carlisle border and two doors down from her sister Joan. In 1988, George purchased and rebuilt that house as their new residence. (The Waite family.)

Charles Parlee began a major restoration and reconstruction of the house and outbuildings. The roofline of the main house changed, as seen here, and the wing for hired help on the right, built by Ezekiel Byam around 1829, became a multicar garage. In 2002, he added a 36-by-36-foot horse stall barn with loft and in 2006 attached a 36-by-48-foot barn to the first. (The Waite family.)

The stables were initially underutilized, but in 2007 Carleen Wilkish from nearby Brush Hill Road started the Midnight Moon Stables. The business hosted clinics and shows, providing care, personalized instruction, and training for hunter and jumper horses. Charles added an insulated 36-by-44-foot stall barn and 81-by-180-foot indoor riding arena in 2012 and 2013 to allow year-round operation. The mare's name is Elementa. (Photograph by the author.)

In 1917, Dorothy Wright purchased this 40-acre farm at 79 Elm Street for her older sister Caroline and father, George C. Wright, a minister at two churches in Lowell. The 1938 hurricane destroyed the barn at right. George died in 1930, but Caroline lived there alone into the 1970s. Dorothy, an advertising executive in Manhattan, met a Scotsman and became Lady Dorothy Pigott of Scotland's Closeburn Castle. (Chelmsford Historical Society.)

Lady Dorothy, then age 86, arranged to sell the property to Dr. Alan Kent of Chelmsford in February 1975. He and his family restored the property and leased the farmland to area farmers, including George Waite and Phillip Jones. The home was placed in the National Register of Historic Places in September 1985, and the open farmland is held in trust by the Kent family. (Monica Kent.)

Four

Nature's Fury

Three natural disasters hit New England in the first half of the 20th century: an ice storm in 1921, a flood in 1936, which affected all towns along the Merrimack River, and a hurricane in 1938. This photograph shows the aftermath of the 1921 ice storm at Kate's Corner, with buildings, from left to right, Emerson & Co. store, First Baptist Church, and Henry Staveley's blacksmith shop. (Pamela Rivard.)

The Great New England Ice Storm started on November 28, 1921, first with snow then freezing rain, lasting until 31 November. A 1934 *Popular Science* magazine article stated that wires and tree limbs went down over a 3,600-square-mile area, and over a million miles of wire had to be restrung. The Lyman Byam house at 305 Acton Road is at left, looking east toward Chelmsford Center. (Pamela Rivard.)

From left to right, Frank Byam, Lyman Byam, Fred Park (from 12 Park Place), and Frederick Russell inspect the ice damage on Maple Road. Frank's barn at 19 Maple Road is at left, and Daniel Byam's house at 11 Maple Road is to its right, with drooping branches blocking the view toward the First Baptist Church. The storm covered all of central Massachusetts and part of southern New Hampshire. (Pamela Rivard.)

The Lowell Electric Light Corporation's booklet called "The Ice Storm of November 1921" explained that the storm started with wind-driven heavy wet snow that stuck to everything and was followed by rain from a layer of warm air above falling into a cold layer below and freezing. If the rain that fell had been snow, the equivalent snowfall would have been about four feet. From left to right, Frank Byam, Lyman Byam, and Fred Park are in front of Frank's barn complex, with Daniel Byam's house to their right. Frank was the second agent for the New York, New Haven & Hartford Railroad at the station on the other side of Maple Road, with Lyman taking over the job in 1895. The passenger station closed in 1921, the same year as this storm. (Pamela Rivard.)

The Great New England Hurricane of September 21, 1938, hit Byam's Grove on Heart Pond particularly hard. Located on a point of land surrounded by open water, there was little to resist the wind, and with sandy soil, little to keep the roots anchored. Two of Lyman Byam's daughters were in the family camp seen here when the wind picked up. Trees started falling, but the girls were not injured. (Pamela Rivard.)

Pine trees were a large part of the atmosphere at Byam's Grove, and most of the big ones were on the ground after this storm. The bungalow made from two chicken coops, used as sleeping accommodations for family and guests, survived and is in the center above. Sawmills were busy for months afterward, trying to convert the glut of trees into lumber. (Pamela Rivard.)

This is the waterfront on the west side of Byam's Grove looking north. Rental rowboats were tied up on the east side of the point and stored in a garage off-season and were not damaged. With the shady pines down and World War II on the horizon, the campground business dried up, but the family continued to use the rowboats. Byam families still gather at the grove. (Pamela Rivard.)

From left to right, Lyman, Grace, and Evelyn Byam are seated among the fallen trees. Evelyn was one of the daughters surprised by the storm and was the last of the nine children to leave home. The downed trees were so thick and jumbled that Lyman reported having trouble finding his way around his own property. (Pamela Rivard.)

Some of the older trees at 19 Maple Road damaged by the 1921 ice storm survived the 1938 hurricane, but many younger trees did not, as seen in this photograph. Frank Byam lived in Lowell with son Lyman after his wife, Amelia, died in 1925, and after his death in 1933, the farm was purchased by the Blaisdell family, who owned it when the hurricane struck. (Chelmsford Historical Society.)

John and Arthur Scoboria, carpenters and brothers from Cornwall, England, purchased the farm at 47 Proctor Road in 1871. When the hurricane hit in 1938, it was owned by Arthur's three children John P. and Arthur G. Scoboria, and Alice (Scoboria) Lapham. Arthur G. was the town physician for the first half of the 20th century, with his home and office next door to the Adams Library. (Chelmsford Historical Society.)

The Scoboria house at 47 Proctor Road came with about eight acres of land on the west side of the road and a barn complex, seen here, on the east side with about 10 acres of land. Mabel Paignon lived just up the street at 66 Proctor Road and took this photograph after the trees were cut so cars could drive through to South Chelmsford center. (Chelmsford Historical Society.)

Two large trees across from 66 Proctor Road were uprooted by the hurricane. Mabel Paignon lived here in 1938 with her parents Emile and Emma, brothers Arthur and Ray, and sisters Francis and Grace. In the early 1900s, postmasters printed postcards of local scenes for sale at their post offices. Mabel hand annotated her own negatives, like this one, and later many of these were professionally re-annotated. (Chelmsford Historical Society.)

Hans Johnson and his wife, Andrine, emigrated from Norway in 1896, started farming on High Street, and purchased this farm at 176 Hunt Road in 1907. Their youngest son Marvin was born that same year and became the owner of the farm in 1937 just one year before the hurricane passed through. Lori Lane now occupies the site of the barn complex seen here at left. (Chelmsford Historical Society.)

In 1922, William and Alice Wilson from Medford, Massachusetts, purchased this farm at 171 Hunt Road across the street from Hans Johnson and ran it as a truck farm. After the mess seen here in 1938, William started a poultry business, as did many other area farmers in the 1940s and 1950s, but he died in 1943. Alice sold the farm in 1958. (Chelmsford Historical Society.)

Five
GONE FOREVER

This postcard view from 30 Maple Road shows the houses at Nos. 23 and 19 Maple Road on the left, the First Baptist Church at center, and the South School at top right. Below that is the house at 333 Acton Road, the railroad passenger station, the freight house, and the house at 3 Parkerville Road at lower right. The field at upper right is now industrial. (Chelmsford Historical Commission.)

The Lowell & Framingham Railroad, later the Old Colony Railroad line, was constructed in 1871, with Solomon Byam as the first agent at South Chelmsford station. Solomon died in 1873, and his son Frank inherited the 19 Maple Road farm, seen in the photograph below, and took over as station agent across the street. Frank's son Lyman took on the job in 1895 and is seen here at about that time. This station, like thousands of others east of California, was an agency for the American Express Company founded in 1850 by Henry Wells, William Fargo, and John Butterfield. American Express shipped goods, securities, and currency anywhere in the country, sold money orders, and in 1891 copyrighted Traveler's Cheques to replace letters of credit, which were not always honored by foreign banks. (Above, Pamela Rivard; below, Chelmsford Historical Society.)

The Old Colony line was absorbed by the New York, New Haven & Hartford Railroad in 1893, and one of its gondolas is on the freight siding around 1900. This siding later served Eastern States Farmers Exchange, then Agway, under Penn Central ownership until 1976 when Conrail took control and abandoned the line. The tracks were removed when construction of the Bruce Freeman Rail Trail began in 2008. (Don MacGillivray.)

Lyman Byam is standing here with his wife, Grace, around 1921, the year passenger service ended. After this, Lyman commuted to Lowell to work in the railroad yard office there, and in 1926 his son Edwin rented him a house on Stevens Street in Lowell, closer to work. After a few years, he returned home to 305 Acton Road, worked at the Chelmsford Center train station, and then retired. (Pamela Rivard.)

After 1921, Emile Paignon leased the now unused passenger station and freight house from the railroad. His daughter Mabel was appointed postmaster in January 1924, and the post office was set up in the passenger station. Emile ran a hay and grain business in the freight house advertising Wirthmore poultry feeds and Purina chows. He was also a distributor for International Harvester, McCormack, and Deering farm machinery. (Chelmsford Historical Society.)

In February 1956, the railroad dismantled the passenger and freight houses, as seen here. The building on the right was a furniture and toy woodworking shop owned by Edward Whalen of 8 Proctor Road, son-in-law of farmer George Waite. After bankruptcy in 1962, railroad trustees sold the passenger site to developer Ralph House and the freight site to Eastern States Farmers Exchange, which became Agway by 1966. (Chelmsford Historical Society.)

Civil War veteran Samuel Garland and his wife, Susan, raised five children here at 297 Acton Road. Samuel died in 1903, and Susan lived here in 1910 with four of her grandchildren, Ruth, Ethel, and Alexander Park and Elizabeth Byam, seen here. Elizabeth was an honor student at the South School, seen here on the right, and later at Centre School. Sadly, she died in 1915 at only 28. (Pamela Rivard.)

Match manufacturer Ezekiel Byam sold land at 295 Acton Road to the Town of Chelmsford School District 3 in 1853 for school purposes. One condition of the deed was that a six-foot-high fence be maintained around three sides of the 100-by-80-foot lot. The teacher in this one-room schoolhouse changed from term to term, and the students in this photograph were not identified. (Chelmsford Historical Society.)

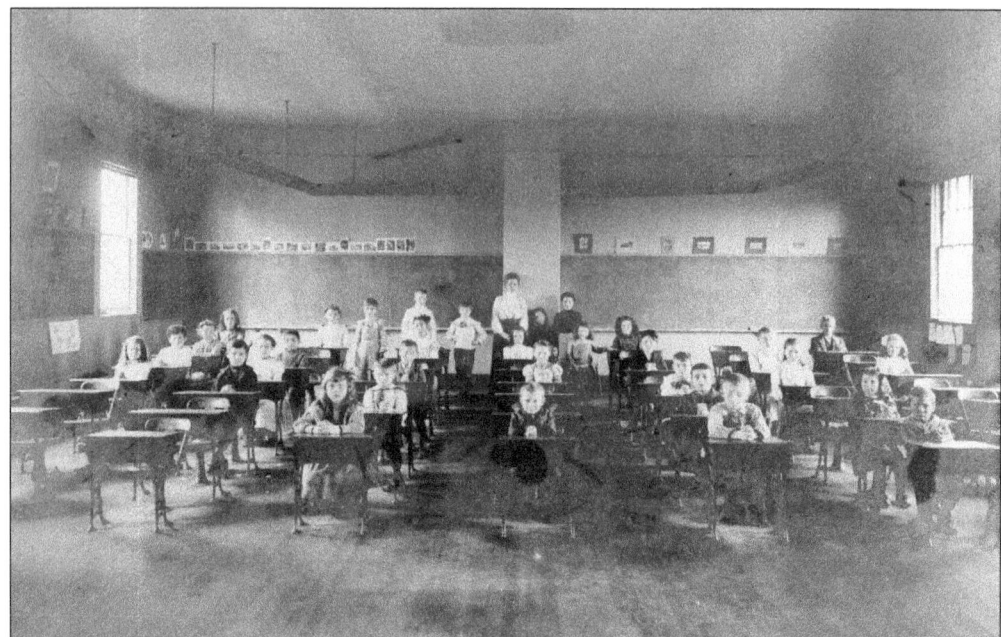

Grace Parkhurst, standing next to the chimney enclosure at the rear of the classroom, taught grades first through sixth here in 1905 and 1906. Students present but not identified included Roy and Rose Paignon, Mildred and Gladys Winning, Nathan and Gertrude Lapham, Glendon Scoboria, Quincy Park, Katherine and Jacob Bogdonoff, and Herbert Penniman. Heat from a stove behind the building was distributed by stovepipes hanging from the ceiling. (Chelmsford Historical Society.)

In 1908, a new school was built at 15 Proctor Road, and the old building turned over to the District 5 volunteer fire company. In 1921, this Ford chemical truck was purchased by the town. The men on the truck, from left to right, are Sidney Dupee, Otis Brown, Horace House, Arthur House, Fred Sargent, and Henry Staveley. The house at 192 Robin Hill Road is at left. (Don MacGillivray.)

The old fire wagon kept in the building was disposed of at auction in 1924, and a new siren was installed on the roof in 1930. The wood floor inside was replaced with concrete in 1934 to accommodate a new Maxim pumper engine purchased that year. Running water was added in 1937, and in 1952 toilet accommodations and heat to keep the plumbing from freezing were installed. (Don MacGillivray.)

The overhead door seen here was installed in 1958. At the 1966 Town Meeting, a building committee was appointed to manage the construction of a new fire station on the same site, and the Board of Selectmen was authorized to dispose of this one. The new station was opened in January 1967, and a permanent firefighter was stationed there around the clock for the first time. (Chelmsford Historical Commission.)

Grace Parkhurst and Ethel Wright taught the last class at the Acton Road schoolhouse in December 1907, and the students started in this new two-room schoolhouse at 15 Proctor Road in January 1908. Emma Graham taught grades first through fourth in one room, and Irene Norton taught grades fifth through eighth in the other. Starting this year, teachers were hired for the entire school year instead of by the term. (Don MacGillivray.)

In this 1938 photograph, students pose on the steps of the South School with teachers Nora Miskell (grades fourth through sixth) and Veronica McTeague (grades first through third), seated left to right at top right. The students, not identified here, were from these local families: Allen, Clark, Durrell, Eliasen, Emanouil (5), Karafelis (3), LaFerriere (2), McHugh (4), Niemaszyk, Parlee (3), Pentedemos, Pond, Reid (3), Vrouhas, and Warren. (Chelmsford Historical Society.)

Enrollment at South School dropped during the 1940s, and in 1952 the building was leased to the Chelmsford Grange. The Grange combined the two classrooms into one large room with a stage and was very active for about 20 years. The Grange gave up its lease in 1976, and it was reassigned to the Girl Scouts, who were among seven organizations applying for use of the building. (Chelmsford Historical Society.)

The Chelmsford Scout House, Inc. was not an official council facility but was run by a group of Girl Scout leaders. They started out with high hopes in 1977, but by 1981, one board of directors' faction was ready to dissolve the corporation, and another was strongly opposed. Out of options for use in 1987, the town held an auction, and it was purchased by two Chelmsford investors. (Linda Prescott.)

The buyers hired contractors to convert the former schoolhouse into a private home, but they failed to get the financing needed to cover costs. Contractor Alan Liguori was looking to build a new home for his family at the time, paid off the investors and subcontractors, and completed the project. It has the exterior look and feel of the original schoolhouse, as seen above in September 2004. (Photograph by the author.)

In 1910, farmer William Reid purchased land on the north side of Littleton Road west of Hunt Road from Mary Byam (of Clarke School for the Deaf fame). He started a filling station in 1932, adding the "finest cabins in New England" by 1940. William sold these businesses at 223–225 Littleton Road to cook Louis Ducharme in 1947 but kept Reid properties at Nos. 215, 221, and 231. (Don MacGillivray.)

Louis Ducharme sold the restaurant and cabins, now named "Dad and the Boys," to Robert Ducharme in 1947. Robert lost the restaurant at a foreclosure auction to William Burns in 1962 and sold the cabin lot to Burns in 1975. The properties at 223–231 Littleton Road were purchased in 2002 by Kensington at Chelmsford LLC and are now an apartment complex by the same name. (Don MacGillivray.)

In 1948, Fred Cahill and Thomas Coyne from New York established Malverne Cabins at 270 Littleton Road, as seen here. Frank and Susan Mason took over in 1954 but the next year started the transition into a mobile home park. The DeCotis family operated the property as Chelmsford Trailer Park, Inc, and more recently, RHP Properties of Farmington Hills, Michigan, operated as the Chelmsford Commons Manufactured Homes Community. (Don MacGillivray.)

Drive-in theater popularity peaked in Massachusetts between 1958 and 1972. Commercial developers Joseph and Sy Solomont, operating as Derry Frosted Foods, purchased 29 acres of land from the estate of James Cormick in 1956. They surveyed a 15.1-acre rectangle at 360 Littleton Road plus a 3.15-acre strip extending along Littleton Road to Garrison Road for an access route to a single-screen drive-in theater. Corporate ownership then passed to Universal Associates, Chelmsford Drive-In, Chelmston, Chelmsco, and the Chelmsford Theater Corporation. The Carpenter Family Corporation purchased the property in 1972 and added a second screen. Residents remember parking in the back rows for romantic evenings where movies like *Galaxy of Terror* and *Humanoids of the Deep* were incidental to the real action. Chelmsford Center was clogged with traffic after the movies wrapped up around 11:30 p.m. (Both, David Paquette.)

Employees remember that before sound was transmitted to car radios, the loss of speaker boxes that hung on car windows was a chronic problem. If a car came in with just one person, it was a good idea to have the driver pop the trunk to see how many people might be hiding there. When a martial arts movie played, the restroom paper towel dispensers were often karate chopped and had to be repaired, and fights would break out for some reason when Mel Brooks's comedy *Blazing Saddles* was played. Drive-in theaters faded with the advent of VCRs and cable television, and the Carpenters closed the Chelmsford Twin in 1988. The property was sold to the Commons Realty Trust for condominium development in October 1989. There were only seven drive-ins still operating in Massachusetts by 1998. (Both, David Paquette.)

Samuel C. Hunt, from a prominent merchant shipping family in Charlestown, Massachusetts, lived here at 93 Hunt Road with his wife, Elizabeth, and their children Eliza, Olive, Hannah, Sarah, Susan, and Henry. In 1867, Eliza and Dr. Theodore Edson of Lowell organized the Parish of St. Anne, which was later renamed All Saints' Episcopal Church. Samuel died in 1878, leaving two houses and 156 acres. Elizabeth died in 1893, and Eliza, Olive, Hannah, and Susan, who were unmarried, stayed on in the house. In 1896, they sold their "Walker place" and its 50 acres of land to wood and ice magnate Daniel Gage. Olive and Susan died in 1906 and 1907, and these October 1907 photographs show that the homestead was in serious disrepair. It became vacant after Eliza and Sarah died in 1912 and 1913. (Both, Chelmsford Historical Society.)

Frank Crawford purchased 93 Hunt Road in the 1930s, rebuilt the main house, and sold it to Ralph, Emma, and son Stowell Howard in 1951. It is seen here in 1973. Stowell died in 1987, and his heirs sold the property to an investor who defaulted on his mortgage in 1989. The house was sold at auction in 1990, demolished in 1991, and replaced with new construction. (Chelmsford Historical Commission.)

The Andrew and Sarah Park farm at 12 Park Place Road, seen here around 1900, was situated on 63.5 acres set back about 180 yards from Park Road. The large barn sits on the edge of the present-day first hole at the Chelmsford Country Club on Park Road. In 1958, Fred, youngest of Andrew's seven children, transferred the property to his children Charlotte and Philip Park. (Chelmsford Historical Society.)

In 1963, Charlotte (Park) DeWolf sold 31.5 acres to cemetery superintendent Archie Jordan, who built a nine-hole golf course surrounding the homestead on three sides. Lowell Electronic Park Realty Trust purchased the golf course in 1972 and sold it to Apple Country Club Inc. in 1979. With the course in danger of being sold for development, the Town of Chelmsford took it by eminent domain in 1995. (Chelmsford Historical Society.)

Charlotte DeWolf was Chelmsford's town clerk from 1957 to 1972 and treasurer and tax collector from 1964 to 1972. This photograph was taken in 1973, and Charlotte passed away in 1999. A trust subdivided the site into three building lots, and the house was torn down in 2005. The parlor interior was removed and placed in a specially constructed exhibit building at the Old Chelmsford Garrison House. (Chelmsford Historical Commission.)

The home of Emile and Emma Paignon at 66 Proctor Road was built by Emma's father, Narcisse Roy, in 1899. They raised nine children here: Rose, Roy, Mabel, Ellen, Arthur, Ida, Grace, Thelma, and Frances. This large and industrious family was well connected to the business life of South Chelmsford. The houses at 47 and 43 Proctor Road can be seen on the left. (Chelmsford Historical Society.)

In 1968, the surviving seven Paignon children sold 66 Proctor Road to Endmoor Development Corporation. A subdivision plan was drawn with four lots along Proctor Road with addresses 66, 68, 70, and 72 and a break between 70 and 72 that later became Buttercup Lane. The Paignon homestead was demolished in 1968, and unmarried siblings Arthur, Grace, and Mabel built a new home at 55 Proctor Road. (Chelmsford Historical Society.)

The Pierce family, who count Pres. Franklin Pierce among their relations, owned land since Stephen Pierce Jr. purchased two lots of subdivided Indian Wamesit land from Thomas Hinchman around 1696. Irish immigrant John McKennedy purchased a 9.4-acre parcel at 62 Riverneck Road from Orrin Pierce in 1882, constructing this house and barn in 1895. John McKennedy's grandson James continued the family farming tradition until about 1982. (Photograph by the author.)

In 1984, James McKennedy sold 12.54 acres of farmland west of Route 3, now part of the Apollo Drive industrial complex. In 2012, the time came for his son Dennis to sell the 62 Riverneck Road farm. A two-year effort by the Chelmsford Historical Commission failed to save the home from demolition, and it was replaced by Alyssa Way with 14 new construction residences. (Photograph by the author.)

Six
East Chelmsford

Irish farmer Charles Finnick purchased land in 1883 and 1896 and with his wife, Mary (McKennedy) Finnick, built this home at 105 Carlisle Street. Of their 11 children, Michael was the last heir, and his estate was sold to Thomas and Dorothy Firth in October 1954. The Firths ran a turkey farm on the property and operated a stand next door at 131 Gorham Street. (Gary Frascarelli.)

Radio personality and ice cream aficionado Gary Frascarelli purchased the 131 Gorham Street farm stand in 1973, opening Gary's Ice Cream stand for sales and production. Gary worked at Glennie's on Pawtucket Boulevard (now Heritage Farm) in the 1960s, becoming an expert on ice cream flavoring and manufacturing, and later opened several stands of his own. He purchased the 105 Carlisle Street house in 1978 as his residence. (Gary Frascarelli.)

Joseph and Maria Ferreira from Camacha, Madeira, Portugal, arrived in the United States in March 1913. Joseph's son Anthony, fourth of nine children, purchased the Gorham Street Filling Station at 15 Gorham Street around 1950, but it later turned out to be in the path of Route 495 and was demolished in 1959. Anthony needed a new location for his service station business. (Christopher Ferreira.)

Joseph Ferreira's brother Manuel emigrated from Madeira in 1914, and in the 1920s they purchased adjacent properties on Riverneck Road starting near the McKennedy farm, crossing Marshall Street, and ending at St. Joseph Cemetery. In 1961, Anthony purchased a lot from his parents at the corner of Riverneck Road and Marshall Street and built Tony's Garage, as seen here. His son Michael is in the wrecker around 1967. (Christopher Ferreira.)

Anthony's three sons, John, Andy, and Michael, worked with him until 1973, when Andy started Ferreira's Towing and transport service on Route 110. Michael died unexpectedly at 45 in 2005, and his nephew Christopher became the owner of Tony's Garage and Christopher's Emergency Equipment and Towing. The cable winch and boom seen on this Mack R-600 and the others above became obsolete after 1975, when hydraulic systems became affordable. (Christopher Ferreira.)

Deacon Otis Adams owned a large parcel of land on Riverneck Road and had a subdivision surveyed in 1892 with five streets and 293 lots. The 2,500-square-foot lots were very small and never sold individually. Gussie Stewart, whose husband, John, died around 1895, purchased 22 lots in 1896 and seven more in 1897, all in a continuous block, and built the estate seen here. (Chelmsford Historical Society.)

Gussie Stewart is seen here around 1900 with friend Samuel Hines and daughter Lydia on the porch. Gussie married Samuel in 1901. Only Monmouth Street survives from the original subdivision, and each of its nine homes were built on multiple lots. Trenton, Lexington, Concord, and Eutaw Streets were never built, and the western end of the subdivision was eventually purchased for expansion of Pine Ridge Cemetery. (Chelmsford Historical Society.)

George C. Moore constructed two large barns by 1919 as part of his Nabnasset farm, formerly his Nabnasset Grove recreation facility, in Westford. After his death, the larger one was repurposed for theatrical performances and movies, as seen here, and then became home of the Nabnasset Lake Country Club. Around 1950, the club decided to downsize by removing the larger barn and moving into the smaller one. (Richard McLaughlin.)

Anthony Sears emigrated from Portugal in 1890 and purchased a farm near 22 Marshall Street in 1919. He purchased adjacent parcels in 1950 and 1951 and, needing a larger barn, reassembled the upper floor of the Nabnasset Lake Country Club barn above a new first floor constructed with concrete blocks, as seen here. The farmland was sold by Sears heirs in 1985 for a 71-lot development. (Richard McLaughlin.)

Francis and Catherine Loucraft ran a store in their farmhouse at 114 Gorham Street starting in 1922, and two subsequent owners maintained a business there. Wilfred and Anita Pare from Lowell, seen here in 1938, purchased the farm in 1947 and ran a grocery store in the house. Gorham Street, now designated as Route 3A, was Route 3 then, a heavily traveled main road from Boston to Lowell. (Ronald Pare.)

The front of the house faced south instead of toward the road, as was common in older farmhouses. Seven-year-old Ronald Pare is standing on the porch. Before high school, he helped his parents in the store, but during high school, he worked at the Chevron service station next door at 118 Gorham Street. He later leased and then purchased the station, the first of many business ventures. (Ronald Pare.)

This is Pare's store facing Gorham Street with advertising for Sealtest ice cream and Coca-Cola. The opening of the new State Route 3 in 1955 reduced traffic flow, and competition from larger grocery stores led to the closing of the store in 1968. Ronald's father, Wilfred, died in 1977, and in 1984 his mother, Anita, was provided an apartment for life in the rear of the building. (Ronald Pare.)

The barn seen here was one of two barns on the original farm, but the single-story addition is more recent. Sydney "Frank" Hooper formed the Wayside Warehouse in the barn around 1951 with business owner Herbert Marshall from Billerica. One memorable product sold in 1951 was a television with a magnifying glass in front to increase the apparent screen size. The store was renamed Chelmsford Appliance around 1958. (Ronald Pare.)

In December 1973, the "Sales with Service" signs were painted over, but advertisements for refrigerators, gas appliances, and washing machines appeared in the *Lowell Sun* through 1981. Appliance salesman Frank Hooper had a degree in philosophy from Dartmouth, left Harvard law school due to World War II, and later became a pioneer in the mass sale of major appliances. He lived almost 100 years, according to his 2011 obituary. (Ronald Pare.)

In an era before recycling became the norm, old trade-in appliances were stockpiled behind the store for convenience and spare parts. From 1982 to 1985, Chelmsford Appliance advertised "Rebuilt Major Appliances Guaranteed." Perhaps this was a way to generate some income from the junk pile. In any case, the business was abandoned in 1985, and owner Ronald Pare started a restoration of the buildings for other commercial uses. (Ronald Pare.)

Anita Pare is standing by the truck while her son Ronald prepares to reroof the addition in 1985. The house on this property was once occupied by the Frost family, who owned the brickyard on Brick Kiln Road in the 1700s. Thomas Marshall, who lived at 61 Carlisle Street and was the brother of Dr. Jonas Marshall from 40 Byam Road, married Hannah Frost here in 1753. (Ronald Pare.)

This is the commercial space at 110 Gorham Street after restoration was completed and the parking lot paved in 1986. The building to the left of the barn is the former East Chelmsford Fire Station, and the house at far left is 103 Gorham Street. Ronald Pare owns a variety of residential and business properties in East Chelmsford, with headquarters at his historic Faulkner Mill in Billerica. (Ronald Pare.)

Manuel Sousa lived on the island of Madeira, an autonomous region of Portugal located about 600 miles southwest of Lisbon, and married Isabel Pereira in 1911. With few job prospects in 1912, he traveled to the United States and found work in a Lowell mill. Isabel arrived in 1913, and with an expanding family, they purchased a home at 115 Gorham Street in East Chelmsford in 1925. (Isabelle McGonigle.)

The entire Sousa family gathered for this photograph in July 1942. From left to right are (first row) John B., Michael, Mary, Alfred, Ruth (Albert's wife), James, Isabelle, Aurelia, and Clarice; (second row) Albert, Manuel J. (father), Isabel (mother), Anthony, Manuel F., and John Roddy (Mary's husband). Manuel J. enjoyed fishing off the rocks at Stage Fort Park in Gloucester, the destination for this outing. (Isabelle McGonigle.)

In 1946, Manuel F. married Mary Ferreira, a member of another large East Chelmsford family originating in Madeira, Portugal. From left to right are (first row, seated) groom Manuel F. Sousa, bride Mary Ferreira, best man Anthony Sousa, and maid of honor Cecelia Ferreira. The setting for this wedding was the lawn at 39 Marshall Street. Ferreira descendants continue to own homes and businesses nearby on Marshall Street and Riverneck Road. (Isabelle McGonigle.)

All 11 Sousa children were present at a family wedding reception on August 11, 1990, and gathered for this photograph. From left to right are (first row) James, Albert, Michael, Anthony, and John; (second row) Alfred, Aurelia, Mary, Manuel, Isabelle, and Clarice. Six of the seven sons served in the military either during World War II or the Korean Conflict; James, born in 1939, was too young. (Edith Sousa.)

James is seen here in 1942, leaning on the family's 1937 Packard. The US Navy hat likely belonged to his brother Anthony, who lived next door to the East School at 20 Albina Street with his wife, Marjorie, after his Navy service. This garage on Carlisle Street, which belonged to 115 Gorham Street, served as the backdrop for many family photographs over the years and still exists today. (Isabelle McGonigle.)

James and John Roddy Jr. are sitting on the running board of their uncle Alfred's 1932 Buick coupe in front of the garage in 1945. The bare-bones homemade tractor to the right of the garage was made from a 1932 Model B automobile manufactured by Ford as a four-cylinder update to the Model A from 1932 to 1934. A chicken coop is to the right of the tractor. (Isabelle McGonigle.)

Clarice and Isabelle, holding Aurelia's son John Callahan, are in the backyard of 115 Gorham Street in 1945. The rear of homes at 117 and 119 Gorham Street are on the right, and all three houses appear to be built using the same architectural plans. In June 1917, the six lots, now 113 through 123 Gorham Street, were surveyed as a subdivision for then landowner Charles Kappler. (Isabelle McGonigle.)

Pare's Store at 114 Gorham Street can be seen here to the left of the house. Isabel stands behind this group at 115 Gorham Street in 1952, and family members, from left to right, are Clarice, Marjorie (Anthony's wife), above their daughter Linda, and Aurelia, above her son John Callahan. Aurelia, Clarice, and their sister Isabelle were all living here with their parents this year. (Isabelle McGonigle.)

This wire cage in the side yard of 115 Gorham Street was built as a hobby project by Albert and his brother Manuel, who bred and raised "ranch" minks for pelts to sell. They also skinned wild mink and muskrats they trapped in local streams. Nephews James and John Jr. Roddy—visiting from Lowell and, in later years, from Pepperell—are leaning on the cage door. (Isabelle McGonigle.)

Pictured from left to right, John Jr. and James Roddy, Clarice Sousa (holding nephew John Callahan), and James Sousa are outside the backyard chicken pen around 1946. John Jr. and James Roddy were children of oldest Sousa daughter, Mary, and her husband, John Roddy. In 1940, Manuel J. Sousa purchased 16 adjacent subdivision lots in between Pleasant and Biltmore Avenues, totaling 40,000 square feet, to raise additional farm animals. (Isabelle McGonigle.)

The Sousa farmland was part of a 17.6-acre parcel on the west side of Carlisle Street that was subdivided in 1924 by the Biltmore Land Company of Providence, Rhode Island. That development failed, with only Biltmore and Pleasant Avenues surviving. There was a preexisting well on the property, and the Sousas built this two-cow barn. John Sousa milks Brownie the cow on his 16th birthday in June 1947. (Isabelle McGonigle.)

John Sousa went to the barn and milked the cow every morning before school. If time permitted, he would collect neighbors' garbage for the pigs. Pictured from left to right are Clarice Sousa, James and Maureen Roddy, Dorothy Bowden (from 113 Gorham Street), and John Roddy Jr. in 1947. There was another shed on the property for a goat to provide milk for lactose-intolerant James. (Isabelle McGonigle.)

Alfred is using a rotary phone around 1954. The rotary dialing system was a technical revolution in its day, replacing the local operator and patch board. A reliable dial mechanism created a stream of contact closures depending on the number selected; it used the same two-wire phone lines; and it worked when the power went out. Switching was accomplished by banks of mechanical relays in an exchange downtown. (Isabelle McGonigle.)

Albert's son Donald Sousa is in the living room around 1954 with grandmother "Mama" Isabel. Isabel and "Papa" Manuel enjoyed watching TV together whenever they got a chance. Manuel contracted bronchitis from a bout with the flu, aggravated by his first job in a Lowell textile mill and later at the Talbot Mill in Billerica, and succumbed to lung problems in September 1964. Isabel died in June 1967. (Isabelle McGonigle.)

Manuel and Mary Sousa lived at 26 Carleton Avenue, and Manuel is seen here in 1963, visiting 115 Gorham Street with three of his five children; from left to right are Manuel, Denis, and Leonard. In 1960, Manuel's siblings James, John, Michael, Aurelia, Clarice, and Isabelle all lived at 115 Gorham Street. In 1963, John married Edith Olsen from North Chelmsford and moved nearby to 81 Carlisle Street. (Isabelle McGonigle.)

John Callahan and uncle Anthony's wife, Marjorie, are dressed up for Easter Sunday in 1963. The Lowell Rendering Company across the Concord River and now part of Baker Commodities, Inc. is at left, and the houses at 117 and 119 Gorham Street are at center and right. The Sousa farmland was divided into house lots at 8 and 10 Pleasant Avenue in 1964 and remained in the family. (Isabelle McGonigle.)

The East School opened in September 1904 with only two rooms: one for grammar and the other for primary students. Two more rooms were added in 1925, and the adjacent property was purchased in 1928 from farmer Henry Shedd for playground purposes. Isabelle Sousa poses here in front of the school in June 1947. The school was shut down in June 1954 but reopened in September 1956. (Isabelle McGonigle.)

This view of the school from Carlisle Street shows the basketball court built by the Chelmsford Recreation Commission on the playground property in 1969. In 1975, the school committee released the East School building to the recreation commission, and it then became the first Chelmsford Community Center. In May 1985, the town sold the East School to the Greater Lowell Council of the Boy Scouts of America. (Chelmsford Historical Society.)

In November 1999, the Boy Scouts of America sold the former school, seen here in 2011, to the Merrimack Education Center Inc. The playground, now known as Harmony Park, was upgraded by volunteers in 2016. The school property changed hands again in June 2018, when purchased by 60 Carlisle Street LLC, later becoming Lowell's Dr. Janice Adie Day School for pre-kindergarten through grade-12 special education. (Photograph by the author.)

Two East Chelmsford dairy farms are represented by these milk bottles. Joseph Jesus emigrated from Portugal in 1906 and raised his family at 50 Canal Street, which is now a part of St. Joseph Cemetery. Manuel and Frank Mello arrived from Portugal in 1900 and 1902 and, in the 1930s, operated at 71 and 75 Brick Kiln Road, now the site of a United Parcel Service (UPS) distribution center. (Kevin Cantrell.)

In February 1922, the town voted $2,850 to purchase land on the Gorham Street Frank Loucraft farm property and build a firehouse. The Lowell Rendering Company plant can be seen across the Concord River at left, and the roof of the Loucraft barn can be seen above the façade of the new building. In July 1922, the town voted $500 to equip the new firehouse. (Chelmsford Fire Department.)

In 1921, a newly appointed board of fire engineers divided the town into five districts, and on the recommendation of an investigating committee, the town acquired all new motorized equipment. This Ford Model T chemical wagon was purchased for District 4, and as a practical measure, the building committee allowed the wagon to be garaged in the new building before it was accepted by the fire engineers. (Chelmsford Fire Department.)

District 4 chief Henry Quinn is driving the Chelmsford Fire Department No. 4 wagon with George McNulty riding on the rear step. The double set of trolley tracks in the foreground ran down Gorham Street to Lowell, where trolley service ended in 1935. The house in the distant field at left has a modern address of 70 Gorham Street, and the Concord River is beyond. (Chelmsford Fire Department.)

Isabelle Sousa is posing here on a rock overlooking the 108 Gorham Street firehouse in June 1947. A roof was added over the electric siren, and pull-up overhead doors replaced the original side openers. Now known as Veterans Hall, the old firehouse was most recently used by Chapter 47 of the Disabled American Veterans, the Merrimack Valley Vietnam Veterans Inc., and American Legion Post 366. (Isabelle McGonigle.)

Visit us at
arcadiapublishing.com